LETTERS OF A SUFI MASTER

FONS VITAE TITUS BURCKHARDT SERIES

Alchemy: Science of the Cosmos, Science of the Soul

Letters of a Sufi Master *(translator)*

Forthcoming
New Editions of

Sacred Art in East and West

Moorish Culture in Spain

Spiritual Key to Muslim Astrology
in the Writings of Ibn 'Arabi

Siena, City of the Virgin

LETTERS
OF A
SUFI MASTER

The Shaykh Al-ʿArabī ad-Darqāwī

Translated by
TITUS BURCKHARDT

FONS VITAE

First edition by Perennial Books Ltd
Middlesex, England

Fons Vitae Edition published 1998
with the permission of Mme Edith Burckhardt

Printed in the United States of America

Library of Congress Catalog Card Number: 98-74023

ISBN-1-887752-16-1

Fons Vitae
49 Mockingbird Valley Drive
Louisville, KY 40207-1366
email: Grayh101@aol.com
website: www.fonsvitae.com

The cover illustration is "a likeness of Shah Hassan Barhana," according to the inscription in the Nasta'liq script on the manuscript. "Shah" means "king" and is the title popularly bestowed by the people (at least in Afghanistan and the Indian subcontinent) on pious men of religion who have renounced the world for God and are shorn of all material yearnings. These are really the true "kings."

Shaykh, or Shah Hassan, who lived during the seventeenth century in the Deccan, in and around present-day Hyderabad, is popularly remembered as a mystic who often did not care too much about his dress and hence was nicknamed "Barhana," which in Persian translates as "naked"—in this case implying carelessly or improperly attired. He is buried on the outskirts of Hyderabad, and as luck would have it, all my mother's paternal ancestors (the Nizam family) from the late eighteenth century onwards are buried around him and have been the custodians of this graveyard.

—Sultan Ghalib al-Quʿaiti
From whose collection of miniatures
this cover was reproduced

Titus Burckhardt wishes to thank Nancy Pearson and Martin Lings for their collaboration in preparing the English MS.

PREFACE

Mūlay[1] al-ᶜArabī ad-Darqāwī, the author of these letters, was the founder of the Darqāwī Order of Sufis, a Moroccan branch of the great Shādhilī Order which was itself founded by the Shaykh Abu'l-Ḥasan ash-Shādhilī in the 13th century A.D.

According to Mūlay al-ᶜArabī's own account, he met his Master, Mūlay ᶜAl al-ᶜImrānī, known as *al-Jamal* (the camel), at Fez in 1767. This Master was himself a disciple of the Shādhilī Shaykh Mulay al-ᶜArabī al-Fāsī.

The spiritual radiation of the Shaykh ad-Darqāwī brought about a sudden great flowering of Sufism in Morocco and Algeria and beyond. This is worth mentioning because scant justice has been done to it by orientalists, who tend to stress a uniform decadence in Islamic mysticism since the end of the Middle Ages.

Several of Mūlay al-ᶜArabī's direct disciples became outstanding Masters themselves, and gave their names to new branches. This must not be considered as a secession from the order. The acceptance of a new name for a *ṭarīqah*[2]

1. "My lord" or "my Patron," a title used in Morocco to denote a descendent of the Prophet. We have transcribed the word here according to its current Moroccan pronunciation rather than its classical Arabic form *mawlāy.*

2. Literally "way," "method," and by extension "order" or "brotherhood."

on the emergence of an eminent Master simply means that this Master has renewed or adapted the method—without changing the constants—in accordance with his own particular original perception of spiritual realities. The full name of the Madanī branch, for example, remains *Aṭ-Ṭarīqat al-Madaniyyat ad-Darqāwiyyat ash-Shādhiliyyah,* but in practice only one name is used: some members of this particular branch call themselves *Madaniyyah,* others call themselves *Shādhiliyyah,* but they are all none the less *Darqāwā,* reciting the litanies of that order, performing its sacred dance (which differs from those of the Shādhiliyyah who are not Darqāwā), and referring to Mūlay al-ᶜArabī ad-Darqāwī as "the Shaykh of our Shaikhs." Amongst those of his disciples whom Mūlay al-ᶜArabī recognised as "autonomous" Shaikhs was Mūlay Muḥammad al-Būzīdī, who was to have succeeded him but who died before him, and whose disciple Aḥmad ibn ᶜAjībah was the author of some remarkable Sufi treatises.

Mūlay al-ᶜArabī himself, who had succeeded his own Master in 1779, lived to be about eighty years old and died in 1823 in Bū Barīh in the mountains north of Fez among the Banī Zarwāl tribe where his family had been established for many generations.

He was succeeded in Morocco by his son Mūlay aṭ-Ṭayyib ad-Darqāwī from whom the present Moroccan head of the order is descended. Another of Mūlay al-ᶜArabī's successors was the Shaykh Muḥammad al-Fāsī, who founded one Darqāwī Zāwiyah[3] in Cairo and another in Colombo. Many if not all the Shādhiliyyah of Ceylon

3. Literally "corner," the name given to the place where the members of an order congregrate.

are in fact Darqāwā and look to the Cairo center of the Fāsiyyah-Darqāwā as being their mother Zāwiyah.

Another successor was the Shaykh Muḥammad Ḥasan Zāfir al-Madanī (the founder of the already mentioned Madaniyyah) who had originally come from Medina in search of a spiritual Master and who had taken guidance from many Shaikhs, until he finally met the founder of the Darqāwā himself. The Shaykh al-Madanī's son, also named Muḥammad Zafir, writing at the end of the last century, tells how his father met Mūlay al-ʿArabī in 1809 and adds: "He took the path from him and his heart was opened under his guidance, and if it be asked who was my father's Shaikh, it was Mūlay al-ʿArabī ad-Darqāwī."

The Shaykh al-Madanī had a large following and founded many Zāwiyahs, the chief of which was at Misurata in Libya where he is buried. He was succeeded by his son who went to Istanbul where it is said that he was the Shaykh of the Sultan ʿAbd al-Hamīd. However this may be, there can be no doubt that he had considerable influence in Turkey, and it was there, in 1879, that he wrote his book on the order, *al-Anwār al-Qudsiyyah,* published in Istanbul in 1884. Another of his father's successors, named ʿAbd al-Qādir, founded a Zāwiyah in Alexandria. These Darqāwā are thus as it were "first cousins" to the Darqāwā of Cairo. But it was no doubt through yet another successor, the Sharīf[4] ʿAlī Nūr ad-Dīn al-Yashruṭī, that the Madanī branch had it widest expansion. This eminent Sufi, who was born in 1793 and died at the age of 105 in 1898, spent several years with his Shaykh at Misurata and then migrated to

4. "Noble," used in the sense of "descendent of the Prophet."

Acre in Palestine. His daughter, Sayyidah Fāṭimah, who lives in Beirut,[5] is thus the child of a man who was born in the 18th century (there must be few others alive today who can make such a claim) and her book about her father and the order in general, *Riḥlah ila 'l-Ḥaqq,* published about 1954, is a precious link with the past. During his long life, which spanned the whole of the 19th century but for two years, this spiritual grandson of the Shaykh ad-Darqāwī founded many Zāwiyahs centered on Acre, the most important of these being at Jerusalem, Damascus, Beirut and Aleppo. Today the order is particularly wide-spread in the Lebanon from where it has also taken root in Mozambique, where it has thousands of members.

But even more than the Madanī-Yashruṭī branch, it is probably the ᶜAlawī branch of the Darqāwā which has given that order its fullest flowering outside Morocco. The Shaykh Aḥmad al-ᶜAlawī was descended from Mūlay al-ᶜArabī by quite a different line from those already mentioned. By the time of his death, in 1934, his disciples in Algeria (including North Africans in Paris and Marseilles), Tunis, the Yemen, Abyssinia, Syria, Palestine and elsewhere were said to be well over 200,000 in number. After his death, under the head of his Damascus Zāwiyah, the late Shaykh Muḥammad al-Hāshimī, ᶜAlawī-Darqāwi Zāwiyas were founded in Aleppo, Homs, Hama, Latakia and Amman. In Aleppo, at some seasons even more than once a week, one may find as many as 5,000 Darqāwā of this ᶜAlawī branch congregated at the tomb of the Prophet Zachariah in the great Omayyad Mosque.

5. EDITOR'S NOTE: As of 1969, when this introduction was written.

The collected letters (*rasā' il*) of al-ᶜArabī ad-Darqāwī were compiled by himself, copied by his disciples and printed many times in Fez, in lithographed script. Titus Burckhardt has made this translation on the basis of two 19th-century manuscripts as well as the lithographed edition.

These letters are still read, with commentaries, in the Zāwiyahs of the Darqāwī line. But the Fez lithographed edition is now difficult to obtain, which partly explains why the letters themselves are almost entirely unknown to Western scholars, and why Brockelmann himself does not mention them; and even if they were more easily obtainable, their great importance might escape the notice of those whose knowledge of the Sufis comes only from reading works of a general nature, for these letters belong to a body of teaching which as often as not remains oral and which is a feature of what might be called "practical Sufism." What a Shaykh has to say to one or more of his disciples concerning the spiritual path he may first deliver by word of mouth and then he may or may not write it down. Mūlay al-ᶜArabī's Master, Mūlay ᶜAlī al-Jamal, was also the author of a collection of letters, but these only exist in one or two manuscripts and have never yet been published.

MARTIN LINGS

EXTRACTS FROM THE LETTERS

EXTRACTS FROM THE LETTERS

If you wish your path to be shortened in order to attain realization swiftly, hold fast to what is ordained (in the Qur'ān) and to what is particularly recommended concerning voluntary observances[1]; learn outer knowledge as is indispensable for worshipping God, but do not linger on it, since you are not required to study this deeply; a deepening of inner knowledge is what you need; and fight against covetousness; then you will see marvels. "Noble character" is nothing else but the *taṣawwuf* of the Sufis, just as it is the religion of religious men. (And may God curse those who lie.)

Likewise, always flee from sensuality,[2] for it is the opposite of spirituality and opposites do not meet. Inasmuch as you strengthen the senses you weaken the Spirit, and vice versa. Hear what happened to our Master (may God be satisfied with him) at the beginning of his journey. He had just threshed three measures of wheat and went to tell his Master he had done so. Lord al-ʿArabī bin ʿAbd Allāh said to him: "If you increase in the realm of the senses, you

1. *Nawāfil* (pl. of *nāfilah*), that is, rites and other observances which are not legally obligatory but which the Prophet strongly recommended.

2. *Al-ḥiss*: sensuality in the broadest sense of the word, i.e. attachment to sensory experience.

diminish in the realm of the Spirit, and if you grow in the latter, you diminish in the former." This is obvious, because so long as you consort with (worldly) people, you will never smell the perfume of the Spirit in them; you will only smell the smell of sweat, and this is because they have been enslaved by sensuality; it has taken possession of their hearts and their limbs; they see their profit only in it, so that they chatter about it, busy themselves with it, rejoice in it alone and can barely drag themselves away from it. And yet many are they who have freed themselves from sensuality in order to plunge into the Spirit for the rest of their lives (may God be pleased with them and let us profit from their blessing, Amen, Amen, Amen). It is as if God (be He exalted) had not given them Spirit (i.e., to worldly people) and yet each one of them is part of it, as the waves are part of the ocean. If they knew this, they would not allow themselves to be distracted from the Spirit by sensory things; if they knew this, they would discover in themselves boundless oceans; and God is our Warrant for what we say.

* * *

Know (and may God be merciful to you) that the *faqīr,*[3] when he exchanges the remembrance of all things for the remembrance (*dhikr*)[4] of God, purifies his servitude, and whosoever serves God in a pure and unmixed way is holy (may the curse of God be on him who lies). So remember

3. *Faqīr*: the poor (implying *al-faqīru ilā 'Llāh* "poor toward God," as in the saying in the Qur'ān : *O men, ye are poor toward God and He is the Rich, the Glorious.* (XXXV, 15). The Persian equivalent of *faqīr* is *dervish*.

4. *Dhikr*: includes the meanings of mention, rememberance, invocation.

only God; be God's alone; for if you are God's, God will be yours and blessed is he who belongs to God so that God is his. Let the mention of God's word—*Remember Me and I will remember you* (Qur'ān II, 147)[5]—suffice to prove the excellence of the remembrance (*dhikr*) of God. And the word which the Prophet (may God bless him and give him peace) spoke on behalf of his Lord: "I am the Companion of him who calls upon Me."[6]

My Master (may God be satisfied with him) used to say to me: "I like what I hear said against you." In the same way, al-ʿArabī ad-Darqāwī likes what he hears said against you—I mean that which kills your egoism and quickens your hearts; but not the contrary, for only the heedless man, the ignorant man, the man whose intelligence is tarnished and whose conscience is obscured, is concerned with that which quickens the ego (*nafs*)[7] and kills the heart.

5. Quotations from the Qur'ān are given throughout in italics, and these will be followed simply by the numbers of chapter and verse, without the word "Qur'ān."

6. This is a *ḥadīth qudsī* (holy utterance) addressed t the Prophet, not as a part of the Qur'ān but as it were in parallel to it. Its transcendence is shown by the fact that God speaks in the first person. Revelations of this category concern more particularly the contemplative way.

7. *An-nafs* is the soul as opposed to the heart (*al-qalb*). It signifies the egocentric, passionate soul. Accompanied by a possesive pronoun, the same word is translated as: myself, thyself, himself. *An-nafs,* the passionate soul and seat of the ego (Sanskrit *ahankāra*) is opposed to the heart inasmuch as the latter is the organ of *ar-rūḥ,* the Spirit. The heart can be compared to the narrowest part of an hourglass, or to the isthmus (*barzakh*) between two oceans, one salt and the other sweet (Qur'an LV, 19 XXIII, 102), which represent respectively the realm of temporal experience and the realm of pure contemplation. It is also said that the heart is the object of a quarrel between its father, the Spirit, and its mother, the passionate soul. If the mother has the upper hand, the heart hardens; if the father is victorious, the heart becomes luminous like Him.

For man has only one heart: as soon as he turns to one side, he turns away from the other, since *God did not create two hearts in the breast of man* (XXXIII, 3). In the same sense, it was said by the venerable Master, Lord Ibn ʿAṭā-Illāh (may God be satisfied with him) that: "To turn toward God is to turn away from the creature and to turn toward the creature is to turn away from God."

One of our brothers said to me: "I am nothing." I answered: "Do not say: 'I am nothing'; neither say: 'I am something.' Do not say: 'I need such and such a thing'; nor yet: 'I need nothing.' But say: '*Allāh,*' and you will see marvels."

Another brother said to me: "How can one cure the soul?" I answered him: "Forget it and do not think about it, for he who does not forget his soul (does not forget himself) does not remember God." So you are unable to conceive that it is the existence of the world which causes us to forget our Lord. What causes us to forget Him is the existence of ourselves, of our ego. Nothing veils Him from us except our concern, not with existence as such, but with our own desires. If we were able to forget our own existence, we would find Him who is the source of our existence and at the same time we would see that we do not exist at all. How can you conceive that man could lose consciousness of the world without losing consciousness of his ego? That will never come to pass.

* * *

You cannot conceive that the *faqīr* could be completely detached from everything and not be in the presence of God; it is impossible, for he whose spiritual aspiration[8] rises

8. *al-himmah*: spiritual will, the resolve that overcomes worldly passion.

above created things reaches the Creator, and to reach Him is to know Him. Therefore, resolutely leave all the things on which you are relying, whatever they may be, and do not trust in them.

> He perishes who is satisfied with anything else in exchange
> for Thee
> And he who reaches out toward what is far from Thee is lost.
> Anything thou abandonest can be replaced
> But there is nothing to replace God if thou abandonest Him.

Let me tell you about how I was once with my brother in God, the devout and noble Ḥasanī Abu'l-ᶜAbbās Aḥmad aṭ-Ṭāhir (may God's mercy be upon him) in al-Qarawīyyīn Mosque. We were both of us deeply wrapped in contemplation when all of a sudden my companion allowed himself to be distracted—or, let us say, to weaken—to the point of falling into chatter like ordinary people. Abruptly and in anger, I said to him: "If you wish to win, strike, and throw (it) out!"

In the same sense I said to another brother: "Strike neither Jew nor Christian nor Muslim, but strike your own soul (*nafs*) and do not cease to strike it until it dies!" You also, my brothers, cast out idle talk completely and without fail, for it is one of the worst temptations and does not become your spiritual station and state. And say only good of people, for as the Prophet (on whom be blessing and peace) says: "He who is not grateful toward men is not grateful toward God." Besides, as we were saying—and God knows best—he who does not take men into account, that is, who does not know them, does not contemplate God either in a perfect way; for the perfect man is he from whom the creature does not hide the Creator, nor the

Creator the creature. Discriminative knowledge does not hide unitive knowledge from such a man, neither does the unitive hide the discriminative. From him, the effect does not hide the cause, nor the cause the effect; from him, religious law (*sharīʿah*) does not hide spiritual truth (*ḥaqīqah*) nor spiritual truth religious law; from him, method (*sulūk*) does not hide inner attraction (*jadhb*), nor inner attraction method; and so on. He has attained the aim; he is the perfect one, the Gnostic; whereas his opposite is the man who is lost. We are not speaking of God's madman (*majdhūb*),[9] transported out of his senses, for he is not lost at all.

*
* *

As the Sufis affirm, there is no approach to God save through the door of the death of the soul. Now we see—but God is wiser—that the *faqīr* will not kill his soul until he has been able to see its form, and he will see its form only after separating himself from the world, from his companions, his friends and his habits.

One *faqīr* said to me: "My wife has got the better of me"; to which I answered: "It is not she but your own soul which has got the better of you; we have no other enemy; if we could kill it, we would kill all our oppressors with one blow. (May the curse of God be upon him who lies)."

*
* *

9. One who is attracted by the divine *Jadhb* (attraction), the spiritual man whose Spirit is continuously absent from the plane of the senses and reason, in such a way that he appears to be a madman or a sleepwalker.

The soul is an immense thing; it is the whole cosmos, since it is the copy of it. Everything which is in the cosmos is to be found in the soul; equally everything in the soul is in the cosmos. Because of this fact, he who masters his soul most certainly masters the cosmos, just as he who is dominated by his soul is certainly dominated by the whole cosmos.

Whenever someone shows hostility toward you, whether he be one of you or not, do not be concerned with yourselves, but with what your Lord has commanded; provided you do not defend yourselves, God will defend you and take care of your cause; but if you do defend yourselves and are concerned with your cause, He will leave it to you to manage it and you will be powerless, for it is God *Who has power over all things.*

The Venerable Master Qāsīm al-Khaṣaṣī (may God be well pleased with him) said: "Pay no attention to him who slanders you, but pay attention to God; He will remove this slanderer from you, for it is He who incites him against you in order to test your sincerity; but many men are mistaken on this question." If you pay attention to him who slanders you, the slander will continue, together with your sin (of distraction from God).

* * *

The *fuqarā'* (pl. of *faqīr*) of ancient times sought only for what could kill their souls (*nufūs,* plural of *nafs*) and bring life to their hearts, whereas we do just the opposite. We seek after that which kills our hearts and enlivens our souls. They strove only to become free of their passions and dethrone their egos; but as for us, what we long for is the satisfaction of our sensual desires and the glorification of our egos, and thus we have turned our backs to the door and our faces to the wall. I say this to you only because I have seen the favors which God lavishes on him who kills his soul and brings life to his heart. Most certainly we are satisfied with less, but only the ignorant is satisfied with not arriving at the end of his journey. I asked myself whether there could be something else, apart from our passions and our egoism, which cuts us off from the divine gifts, and as a third hindrance I found the lack of spiritual longing. For intuition is generally given only to him whose heart is pierced by an intense longing and a strong desire to contemplate the Essence of his Lord. Intuitions of the divine Essence flow into such a man until he is extinguished in that Essence and thus freed from the illusion of any reality other than It, for this is the direction in which the divine Essence leads those whose gaze is fixed continually upon It. On the contrary, he who aspires exclusively to theoretical knowledge or to action does not receive intuition upon intuition; he would not rejoice in it if he did, since his wish is aimed at something other than the divine Essence, and God (may he be exalted) favors each one according to the measure of his aspiration. Certainly, every man participates in the Spirit, just as the ocean has waves, but sensual experience entirely takes possession of most men; it seizes hold of their hearts and limbs and does not allow them to open to the Spirit, because sensuality is the opposite of spirituality and opposites do not meet.

We see besides that the spiritual aim is reached neither by many works, nor by few, but by Grace alone. As the

Saint Ibn ʿAṭā-Illāh says in his *Ḥikam:* "If you were destined to reach Him only after the destruction of your faults and the abandonment of all your claims, you would never reach Him. But when He wishes to bring you back toward Him, He absorbs your quality into His and your attributes into His and thus brings you back by means of what comes to you from Him, not by means of what comes to Him from you."

One of the effects of Divine Bounty, Grace and Generosity is that one finds the Master who can grant spiritual education; without Divine Grace no one would find or recognize him, since, according to the saying of the Saint Abu'l-ʿAbbās al-Mursī, (may God be well pleased with him): "It is more difficult to know a Saint than it is to know God." Again, in the *Ḥikam* of Ibn ʿAṭā-Illāh, it is said. "Exalted be He Who makes His Saints known only in order to make Himself known and Who leads toward them those whom He wishes to lead toward Himself." There is no doubt that the Lord of the inhabitants of Heaven and Earth, our Master, God's Messenger (may God bless him and give him peace) was openly manifested, like a sun on a standard, and in spite of that was not seen by all, but only by some. God veiled him from others, just as He veiled the Prophets (on them be peace) from certain men, and just as He veils the Saints from the men of their time, so much so that they slander the Saints and do not believe them. God's Books testify to this: *Thou shalt see them looking toward thee and they see not* (VII, 197) and: *They said: what kind of a messenger is this, who eats food and walks in the markets* (XXV, 7) and so on, in all the other analogous passages. Two thirds or more of the divine Book tells how the Prophets (on them be peace) were slandered by the men of their time. Among those who did not see God's Messenger (may God bless him and give him peace) was Abū Jahl (God's curse be upon him); he saw in the Messenger only the orphan who had been adopted by Abū Ṭālib. The same applies to the spiritual Master who is simultaneously ecstatic (*majdhūb*) and methodical (*sālik*), who is at the same time both drunk and sober; only a few find him. Now if one finds the Master (he sometimes acts in an unexpected way); sometimes he sees that the disciple's Spirit will be freed by fasting and so makes him fast; at another time, on the contrary, he will make him eat to repletion for the same purpose; now he sees that the disciple will benefit spiritually from an increase of outer activity; at another time, from less activity; at one time, from sleeping; at another time, from staying awake; sometimes he wishes the disciple to avoid people, sometimes, on the contrary he advises him to frequent people; for it may be that the inner light of the disciple has suddenly become too strong for him, so that the Master fears he may lose his reason, like many disciples in the past and in our day who have become mad; this is why the Master may bring the disciple out of his retreat and make him mix with people, in order that his spiritual tension may diminish and he be preserved from madness. In the same way, if the inner light becomes too weak, the Master sends him back into solitude in order that it may acquire force, and so forth; the issue is in God's hands. Spiritual mastery could very nearly have ceased to be manifested for lack of those whose heart is quickened by an ardent desire to follow it; but the divine Wisdom never runs dry.

We see that the spiritual way (*ṭarīqah*) is necessarily maintained by Divine Force and Power, since it comes down through our Masters from God's Messenger (may God bless him and give him peace). As the Saint al-Mursī (may he be pleasing to God) used to say: "No Master makes himself known to disciples unless he has been led to do so by inspirations (*wāridāt*) and unless he has received the authorization of God and of His Messenger." The blessing (*barakah*) of this authorization and the secret it implies is what sustains our cause and safeguards the state of those who adhere to it; but God is wiser.

As to what we were saying about the attachment of the heart to the vision of the Essence of our Lord, no one of us possesses it so long as his soul is not extinguished, wiped out, vanished, gone, annihilated. According to the Saint Abu'l-Mawahib at-Tunisi (may God be satisfied with him): "Extinction is erasure, disappearance, departure from yourself, cessation": and according to the Saint Abū Madyān (may God be well pleased with him): "He who does not die does not see God." All the Masters of the Way have confirmed this. And beware, beware if you believe that our Lord is veiled from us by solid or subtle things: by God, no! illusion (*wahm*)[10] is the only thing which veils Him from us and illusion is empty. As the Saint Ibn ʿAṭā-Illāh says in his *Ḥikam:* "God is not veiled from you by some reality existing apart from Him, since there is no reality

10. *Al-wahm* means both illusion and imagination, that is to say arbitrary imagination which obscures and misleads, whereas *al-khayāl* often designates imagination as a normal faculty of the soul, receptive to archetypal forms; transposed into Vedantic concepts, these are the two aspects, positive and negative, of *Māyā,* which simultaneously veils and reveals.

outside of Him: what veils Him from you is but the illusion that there can be a reality apart from Him."

We observe—but God is wiser—that this extinction takes place, God willing, in the least possible time, by means of a certain method of calling upon the Name of Majesty: *Allāh*. I came upon this method in the work of the Venerable Master, the Saint Abu'l-Ḥasan ash-Shādhilī (may God be well pleased with him). It is mentioned in certain books owned by a learned man amongst our brothers of the Banī Zarwāl, and I also received it from my noble spiritual Master Abu'l-Ḥasan ʿAlī (may God be well pleased with him), in a slightly different, simpler and more direct form. It consists of visualizing the five letters of the Name while saying *Allāh, Allāh, Allāh*. Each time the letters dissolved in imagination, I revisualized them and if they dissolved a thousand times during the day and a thousand times during the night, I continued a thousand times a day and a thousand times a night to revisualize them. This method gave me moments of immense insight when I practiced it for a little more than a month at the beginning of my spiritual path. It brought me great knowledge as well as an intense awe (*haybah*),[11] but I paid no heed to it, occupied as I was in calling upon the Name and visualizing the letters until the month ended. Then a thought forced itself on my attention: "God (be He exalted) says that *He* is *the First and the Last, the Outer and the Inner*" (LVII, 2). To begin with, I turned away from this thought that crept in, resolved not to listen to it, and I continued to do my

11. *al-haybah* is the state the soul experiences in the face of the terrifying Majesty of God.

exercise; but this voice did not leave me alone; it insisted and did not accept my refusal to listen to it, just as I did not accept its way of acting and did not listen to it. But finally, since it would hardly leave me in peace at all, I answered it: "As for His words saying that He is the First and the Last and that He is the Inner, I understand them quite well; but I do not understand His affirmation that He is the Outer, because all I see on the outside are created things." To this the voice answered: "If by His expression 'the Outer' He meant something other than the outer world which we see, it would not be outside, but inside (that we would have to look for it). But I say to thee: He is the Outer." Then I realized that there is no reality save God and nothing in the Cosmos but Him, praise and thanks be to God.

Extinction in the Essence of our Lord comes about quite quickly, God willing, by the method just described, for by this method meditation bears fruit from the morning to the evening, provided suspension of thought has been practiced long enough. In my case, it bore its fruit after one month and a few days, but God knows best. Certainly if someone were to practice suspension of thought for a year or two or even three, the thought which would result thereafter would attain great good and a dazzling secret.[12]

12. It may perhaps be useful to be reminded at this point that there can be no question of practicing spiritual excercises outside the traditional form to which they belong and the conditions created by it; to do so would be to expose oneself to grave dangers. If the author of these letters speaks of realization coming about "in a short time" (Shankara expresses this in a similar way), it means he has in mind spiritual aptitude (in those he is addressing) the equivalent of which one would no doubt look for in vain in our day.

From this I understood the prophetic saying: "Better an hour of meditation than seventy years of religious practice," since by this kind of meditation a man is transported from the created world into the world of purity; and one could also say, from the presence of the created into the presence of the Creator. And God is our Warrant for what we say.

We recommend to everyone coming back from the state of forgetting (*ghaflah*)[13] toward the state of remembering (*dhikr*) that he fix his heart continually on the vision of the Essence of his Lord, in order that It may pour out Its truths on him, as It does for him whose heart becomes attached to It; and let him not allow himself to be distracted from his invocation by intuitions, lest this prevent him from reaching the aim.

*
* *

The sickness afflicting your heart, *faqīr,* comes from the passions which pass through you; if you were to abandon them and concern yourself with what God ordains for you, your heart would not suffer as it suffers now. So listen to what I say to you and may God take you by the hand. Each time your soul attacks you, if you were to be quick to do what God orders and were to abandon your will entirely to Him, you would most certainly be saved from psychic and satanic suggestions and from all trials. But if you begin to reflect in these moments when your

13. *al-ghaflah* is negligence, unconsciousness or forgetfulness, as opposed to spiritual awakening and the present remembrance of God (*dhikr*).

soul attacks you, to weigh the factors for and against, and sink into inner chatter, then psychic and satanic suggestions will flow back toward you in waves until you are overwhelmed and drowned, and no good will be left in you, but only evil. May God guide us and you on the path of His Saints, Amen.

The Venerable Master, the Saint Ibn ʿAṭā-Illāh says in his *Ḥikam*: "Since you know that the Devil will never forget you, it is your business not to forget Him who *grasps you by the forelock.*" (XI, 56).[14] And our Master used to say: "The true way to hurt the enemy is to be occupied with the love of the Friend; on the other hand, if you engage in war with the enemy, he will have obtained what he wanted from you and at the same time you will have lost the opportunity of loving the Friend." And we say: All good is in the remembrance (*dhikr*) of God, and the only way that leads toward Him is through renunciation of the world, keeping apart from people, inner and outer discipline. "Nothing is more useful to the heart than solitude, thanks to which it enters the arena of meditation," as the Venerable Master Ibn ʿAṭā-Illāh says in his *Ḥikam*. And we say: Nothing is of more profit to the heart than renunciation of the world and the fact of being seated between the hands of God's Saints.

Dethronement of the ego is a necessary condition, according to us and according to all the Masters of the Way, and in this respect one of them said: "The very thing you

14. Grasp of the forelock: an Arabic idiom, referring to a horse's forelock. The man who grasps it has complete power over the horse and for the horse the forelock is as it were the crown of his beauty, the sum of his power of self-assertion.

fear from me is what my heart desires." But you, *faqīr,* should not say this before having said it to your own soul and having forced it to follow this road and no other.

* * *

Nothing makes us so vulnerable to psychic and satanic attacks as concern for our sustenance. And yet our Lord (be He exalted) vowed to us by Himself: *Your sustenance and all ye have been promised is in Heaven; by the Lord of Heaven and earth, this is as true as it is true that ye have speech* (LI, 21–22). And he also said: *Prescribe prayer for thy people and be constant therein. We ask thee not to provide sustenance; We will provide for thee and it is piety that will gain the issue.* (XX, 132). The same meaning is to be found in many other passages from the Qur'ān as also in many sayings of the Prophet (may God bless him and give him peace). There is also the saying of the Saint Abū Yazīd al-Bistāmi (may God be well pleased with him): "My part is to worship Him, as He commanded me, and His part is to feed me as He promised me," and so forth. I mention all this only because I am afraid you may lapse into the misfortune that afflicts most men. For I see them busy with many activities, religious as well as worldly, and fearing nothing so much as poverty. If they knew what riches are to be had from being occupied with God, they would forsake their worldly activities entirely and busy themselves with Him alone, that is, with His commandments. But in their ignorance they keep on increasing their worldly and religious activities while remaining uneasy from fear of poverty or from fear of creatures, which is serious forgetfulness and a deplorable state; and this is the state in which the majority of people

—almost all—exist; may God preserve us from it! Therefore be on guard, my brother, and devote yourself entirely to God; then you will see marvels. Do not give yourself up to the world as most people do, lest you be afflicted with the same misfortune. By God, if our hearts were close to our Lord, the world would soon come toward us and even into our homes, let alone to our doors; for our Lord (be He exalted) says to it: "O world, serve those who serve Me and render weary those who serve you!" By God, if we belonged to our Lord, the entire cosmos and all that it contains would soon belong to us as it has belonged to others, for God would have made the world our servant, inasmuch as He had made us His servants. But we have put that of which we ourselves are lords and masters in the place of our Lord and Master (be He exalted) and are not ashamed of it; "There is no strength and no power save through God!"[15] Our attention should be devoted to religious activities at all times and today more than ever, for in these days one might well imagine that no such thing as religious activity without worldly attachment had ever existed; nevertheless it certainly has existed even if it exists no longer; God bears witness to what we say. We observe (but God knows best) that in these days no one is able to say to the multitude of believers: "reduce your worldly activities and increase your religious activities; God will replace you (in your business) as He has done for others." Today nobody will listen to you—and God knows best—unless you say: "cultivate (your fields), earn, trade" and so forth. But if you say: "leave it, abstain

15. A saying much recommended by the Prophet.

(from the world) and be content," there are very few, even among the elect, who will listen to you—the others even less. Hear what the Saint Abu'l-ᶜAbbās al-Mursī (may God be pleased with him) has said about this: "Other people have their business, but our business is faith in God, fear of God; God (be He exalted) has said: *If the people of the towns had but believed and feared God, we would indeed have opened up to them the blessings of Heaven and of earth* (VII, 94); and at another time the Saint said: "Other people have their affairs, and our affair is God."[16]

*
* *

As to this professor you told me about who is unable to find the state of presence,[17] tell him not to look toward the past nor toward the future, to become the son of the moment, and to take death as the target before his eyes. Then he will find this state, God willing.

We said to one of our brothers: Let him who wishes to be in a perpetual state of presence restrain his tongue. And we advise you: if you are in a state of perplexity (*ḥayrah*),[18]

16. It is interesting to compare the advice given in this letter with that contained on p. 68, referring to the conditions of retreat (*tajrīd*) from the world.

17. *Ḥudūr*: the state of presence before God, concentration on God.

18. *Ḥayrah*: Dismay or perplexity in the face of a situation apparently without issue; or again, in the face of truths which cannot rationally be reconciled; a mental crisis, when the mind comes up against its own limit. If we understand *ḥayrah* on the mental plane, the advice given here by the Shaykh ad-Darqāwī is reminiscent of the Zen method of the *koan*, that is of persistent meditation on certain paradoxes in order to provoke a mental crisis, an utter perplexity, which may open out into supra-rational intuition.

do not hasten to cling to anything, either by writing or by anything else, lest you close the door of necessity with your own hand, because for you this state takes the place of the supreme Name; but God is wiser. Ibn ʿAṭā-Illāh says in his *Ḥikam*: "Sudden distress heralds feast days for one who aspires"; and again: "Distress is the key to spiritual gifts"; and again: "You will perhaps find a benefit in distress which you have not been able to find in fasting nor in prayer; therefore when it descends upon you, defend yourself no longer and do not be concerned with searching for some remedy, lest you drive away the good which comes toward you freely, and give up your will entirely to your Lord; then you will see marvels." Our Master used to say when someone was overcome with dismay: "Relax your mind and learn to swim."

*
* *

Do not give nourishment to all that arises in your heart, but throw it far away from you and do not be concerned with fostering it, forgetting your Lord the while, as most people do, thus going astray, wandering, losing their way in a mirage; if they understood, they would say: what an astonishing thing the heart, in one instant it gives birth to countless sons, some legitimate, others illegitimate and yet others whose nature one cannot discern . . . How then could anyone who spends his time feeding all this offspring be available for his Lord? What a sorry creature this son of Adam, who effaces the Cosmos until not a trace of it remains and whom the Cosmos in its turn will obliterate until not a trace of him remains, save a faint odor which in a little while fades away altogether.

If you love your Lord, *faqīr,* leave your self and your world and people, except the man whose state uplifts you and who shows you God by his words. But beware, beware lest you allow yourself to be deceived by someone, for how many are they who appear to be preaching for God when in reality they are only preaching for their desires. The celebrated Saint, Sayyidī Abū 'sh-Shitā, (may God let us obtain profit through him) says in respect to this: "By God, we call 'My Lord,' or 'Son of my Lord,' only him who cuts off our fetters." The fact is not hidden from you, *faqīr,* that what imprisons a man in this world, which is the world of corruption, and holds him fast, is nothing but illusion (*al-wahm*); but if a man gets rid of this illusion, he passes into the world of purity from which he came; and God brings every stranger back to his homeland.

Certainly all things are hidden in their opposites—gain in loss and gift in refusal, honor in humiliation, wealth in poverty, strength in weakness, abundance in restriction, rising up in falling down, life in death, victory in defeat, power in powerlessness and so on. Therefore, if a man wishes to find, let him be content to lose; if he wishes a gift, let him be content with refusal; he who desires honor must accept humiliation and he who desires wealth must be satisfied with poverty; let him who wishes to be strong be content to be weak; let him who wishes abundance be resigned to restriction; he who wishes to be raised up must allow himself to be cast down; he who desires life must accept death; he who wishes to conquer must be content to be conquered and he who desires power must be content with impotence. Which is to say, let him who wishes to be free rejoice in servitude, as his Prophet, friend and

Lord (God bless him and give him peace) rejoiced in it; let him choose it as the Prophet chose it and not be proud nor rebel against his condition, for the servant is the servant and the Lord is the Lord. . . .

* * *

By God, if we were to leave the world, in the end it would seek us out and find us, as we have sought after it and been unable to find it; it would run after us and come to meet us, as we have run after it and failed to meet it; it would weep over us and we would need to console it, as we have wept for it without finding consolation in it; it would yearn for us and need us, as we have yearned for it when it had no need of us; and so forth.[19] God is our Warrant for what we say. It is said that the world comes, despite itself, to him who is sincere in his asceticism and that if a cap falls from heaven it will fall on the head of him who does not wish for it.

The state of the elect, *faqīr,* consists of virtue, beauty, measure and equilibrium; it is like a bride of incomparable beauty yet who will be enjoyed only by him who has rid himself of passion, in such a way that he has replaced surfeit by hunger; speech by silence; sleep by wakefulness; honor by humiliation; eminence by lowliness; wealth by poverty; strength by weakness; power by powerlessness; or, in a word, by a man in whom the blameworthy qualities have been replaced by the praiseworthy qualities. He it is who will enjoy the bride's beauty, her goodness and all the

19. In Arabic, the term *dunyā,* which denotes the world in the sense "the world here below," is feminine.

wealth of her virtue; he it is who will see his Lord (be He exalted) and his Prophet (may God pray over him and give him peace); let him but purify his heart of all blameworthy qualities and, as we were saying, and God willing, all his wishes will be fulfilled.

Greetings.

*
* *

A strong man is one who rejoices to see that the world is slipping from his hands, leaving him and fleeing from him; who rejoices that people despise him, and speak ill of him and is satisfied with his knowledge of God. The Venerable Master, the Saint Ibn ᶜAṭā-Illāh (may God be well pleased with him) says of this, in his *Ḥikam*: "If the fact that people turn away from you or speak ill of you causes you suffering, return toward the knowledge of God in you; if this knowledge is not sufficient, then lack of satisfaction in the knowledge of God is a far greater trial than that people speak ill of you. The purpose of this slander is that you should not rely on people; God wishes to bring you back from all things so that nothing may distract you from Him."

*
* *

It is said that by the invocation of God (*dhikru 'Llāh*) a believer attains such peace of soul that the great terror on Resurrection Day cannot sadden him; how then could he be disturbed by whatever trials and misfortunes may befall him in this world? So be constant in the invocation of your Lord, my brother, as we have advised you, and you will see marvels; may God fill us to overflowing with His grace. Now in our view, invocation does not mean that a man is forever repeating *Allāh, Allāh* and praying and fasting and then, as soon as misfortune strikes him, runs to right and left looking for remedies and is in despair because he cannot find one. For men who have come to know the Truth (may God be well pleased with them), invocation demands that he who calls on God should abide by the laws that are strictly prescribed, the most important of which is that he should pay no attention at any time to what does not concern him. Then, if his Lord makes Himself known to him, or let us say reveals Himself under one of His names whether of majesty or of beauty,[20] such a man will recognize Him and not fail to know Him. This is true invocation as practised by those who remember God and not the state of him who is constantly occupied in worshipping God and yet, when his Lord reveals Himself in some form opposed to his wish, entirely fails to recognize Him.

* * *

There are many signs by which he who has reached God may be recognized, namely in that all things, great or small, are in his hand and under his control, for he is to the universe what the heart is to the body (but God knows best). When the heart is moved, the limbs move also, and when it is still, they likewise are still; if it arises, they arise; if it sits, they sit; if it becomes contracted, so do they contract; if it relaxes, they also relax; if it weakens, they weaken; if it is strong, they are strong; if it is humble, they

20. Or of the rigor (*jalāl*) or mercy (*jamāl*)

become humble; if it is proud, they become proud, and so forth. In the same way, he who has made his way to God, who has died to himself in contemplation of God's Infinity and freed himself from the illusion that there is any reality other than God—such a man finds that existence follows him and obeys him; wherever he turns, it turns. And God is our Warrant for what we say.

* * *

The Spirit (*rūḥ*) is luminous by nature and issues from the very essence of Light (but God knows best). Now it is known without any doubt that God "grasped a portion of His Light and said to it: 'Be Muḥammad!' "[21] This is how It (the Spirit) became and from its light all things were created; understand this. And the Spirit is nothing other than the soul (*nafs*), which became troubled only because it came to depend on the world of corruption; if it were to forsake this world and be separated from it, it would return to its native land whence it came, that is, to the Dominical Presence.[22] The venerable Master, the Saint Abū Yazīd ᶜAbd ar-Raḥmān 'l-Majdhūb,[23] said, concerning the soul:

> Whence comest thou, who art gifted with spirit,
> Spiritually with love,
> Motionless amid the unfolding of thy glory,
> Lordly in all thy states?

And if you were to say to me: "Our Master, the Lord ᶜAlī, (may God be well pleased with him) was broad, while

21. Saying of the Prophet.
22. See p. 46, note 30.
23. "God's madman," a surname given to the famous Moroccan Sufi of the 16th century; one of the "poles" of the Shādhilī initiatic chain.

you are narrow," I would answer: he was broad and narrow to an equal degree; he was both gentle and rough, strong and weak, rich and poor; he was an ocean without shores. His knowledge was sweeter than sugar, more bitter than the colocynth. For he was always repeating these words of the Saint Abū'l-Mawāhib at-Tūnisī: "If anyone claims that it is possible to contemplate divine Beauty without having been schooled by divine Rigor, throw him out, for he is an antichrist (*dajjāl*)" . . .

*
* *

When the servant knows his Lord, all creatures acknowledge him and all things obey him. But God knows more.

The illustrious Shaykh our Master (may God be well pleased with him) used to say: "When your heart is emptied of beings it becomes filled with Being and from that moment love is born between you and other beings. If you act purely toward your Creator, all creatures will manifest goodwill toward you." And we will add: when you are sincere in contemplation of your Lord, He will try you by manifesting Himself to you in all His aspects and if you continue to recognize Him and do not ignore Him, then the universe and all it contains will recognize you; it will love you and behave toward you with veneration and generosity; it will rally to your side, obey you and want you; it will rejoice in remembering you, show concern for you, be glorified in you, flock toward you, call you; all this you will see with your own eyes. But if you fail to know God when He manifests Himself to you, you also will be unrecognized by all things, denied by all things, humiliated, despised, diminished, made more despicable, worse, heavier, more remote; everything will insult you, shun you, be against you and overwhelm you.

You who are "poor," if you wish that your wind may prevail over all winds and all adversaries, then be constant in contemplating your Lord while He is trying you, for He will change your ignorance into knowledge, your weakness into strength, your helplessness into power, your poverty into wealth, your lowliness into glory, your loneliness into intimacy, your remoteness into nearness—or, in a word, God, be He exalted, will cover over your qualities with His qualities, for He is generous and bestows immeasurable graces.

Greetings of Peace!

*
* *

By God, my brothers, I did not believe that a learned man could deny the vision of the Prophet (God bless him and give him peace) in the waking state, until the day I met some learned men in the Qarawiyyīn Mosque and had a conversation with them on this matter. They said to me: "How ever is it possible to see the Prophet when one is awake, since he has been dead for over 1,200 years? It is only possible to see him in a dream, since he himself said: 'He who sees me, that is to say in a dream, sees me in reality, for the Devil cannot imitate me.'" I answered: "Of necessity, he can be seen in the waking state only by one whose mind—or let us say, whose thoughts—have transported him from this corporeal world into the world of Spirits; there will he see the Prophet without the slightest doubt; there he will see all his friends." They were silent and said not a word when I added: "Indeed he can be seen in the world of Spirits." But after a while they said to me. "Explain how this is so." I answered: "Tell me yourselves where the world of Spirits is in relation to the world of bodies." They did not know what to reply. And then I said: "There where the world of bodies is, there also is the world of Spirits; there where the world of corruption is, there also is the world of purity; there where is the world of the kingdom (*mulk*), there also is the world of kingship (*malakūt*); in the very place where the lower worlds are, there are to be found the higher worlds and the totality of worlds. It has been said that there exist ten thousand worlds, each one like this world, (as recounted in the 'Adornment of the Saints')[24] and all these are contained in man, without his being conscious of it. Only he whom God sanctifies by absorbing his qualities into His own, his attributes into His own, is conscious of this. Now, God sanctifies many of his servants and does not cease from sanctifying them until their end."

The venerable Master and Saint, Lord Ibn al-Bannā (may God be well pleased with him) says in his "Inquiries":

> Understand, for thou art a copy of Existence
> For God, so that nothing of Existence is lacking in thee.
> The Throne and the Pedestal, are they not in thee?
> The higher world and also the lower world?
> The Cosmos is but a man on a big scale,
> And thou, thou art the Cosmos in miniature.

And the venerable Master, the Saint al-Mursī (may God be well pleased with him) said:

24. *Hilyat al-awliyā'*, by Abū Nuʿaym al-Isbahānī

O thou who goest astray in the understanding of thine own
secret,
Look, for thou shalt find in thee the whole of existence;
Thou art the Infinite, seen as the Way and seen as the Truth,
O thou synthesis of the Divine Mystery in Its Totality.

*
* *

If you wish what you need to be given to you without your having to search for it, turn away from it and concentrate on your Lord; you will receive it if God wills. And if you gave up your needs entirely and were occupied only with God, He would give you all the good things you wish for in this world and in the other; you would walk in Heaven as well as on the earth; and more than that, since the Prophet (on him be blessings and peace) has said, in the very words of his Lord[25]: "He who by remembering Me (*dhikr*) is distracted from his petitionaaa will receive more than those who ask."

Hear, *faqīr,* what I said to one of our brothers (may God be well pleased with them): every time I was lacking something, great or small, and turned away from it in turning toward my Lord, I found it there in front of me, thanks to the power of Him who hears and knows. We see that the needs of ordinary people are filled by paying attention to them, whereas the needs of the elect are filled by the very fact that they turn away from them and concentrate upon God.

Greetings of Peace!

*
* *

25. *Ḥadīth qudsī* (See p. 17, note 6).

There was a man who came to visit us off and on over a period of about eight years; his attitude toward us varied; at times his love increased, then again it grew weaker.

One day in conversation with him we spoke in a way that touched him to the very heart (but God knows best). From that moment he turned away somewhat from the world and came closer to us in a burst of enthusiasm. Then it happened that he was flooded by spiritual insights, although he had no previous experience of this, and they became so strong that he imagined there was no man on earth wiser than he.

We lived some distance apart and he ran straightway to share his knowledge with us. When he had spoken and we answered him, he flatly contradicted us, hurling his words in our face and becoming angry; all this in the presence of a gathering of brothers (may God be well pleased with them). Since he had never behaved like that to us before, we forgave him, but he did not forgive us and continued to fight against us with his new knowledge. There in front of him we sat as if we were a robber and his band. However, we did not agree with what he said except in part, that is, except insofar as we felt he was right. After having given us the benefit of his discoveries, he left us and went off to some brothers who, though well and lovingly disposed toward us, yet lacked spiritual strength and so were dependent on theory alone. He unsettled them in their intention, their love and their sincerity, and almost succeeded in leading them away from their religious aim and sincere devotion.

Now he tried to persuade us that we ought to leave our seclusion (*tajrīd*) and return to activity in the world.

To this we replied: "For our part, if we were to return as you suggest, we would do so without loss of power, for all of us know the one side and the other (the world and the Spirit); but what is necessary in your case is only to flee from sensuality[26] lest you fall back into it, as many like you have done, many even whose spiritual state was far stronger than yours. Beware, if you wish your soul to be saved: listen to what I am saying and follow it; may God take you by the hand. Sensuality, my brother, is still very close to you, since, as for most people, it is the only thing you know. The majority of people know the sensory world only and not the spiritual world, nor the way leading to it. Now if you wish to follow that way, flee from sensuality, as we have fled from it; strip yourself of it, as we have stripped ourselves; fight it as we have fought and walk on the path that we have trod. My brother, if you wish for sensory things, you do not desire the spirit and your heart is not attached to it, for everything that strengthens the senses weakens spirituality and vice versa . . ." But he did not accept our words and, just as we had warned him, sensuality stole away the spiritual insight that had possessed him, leaving him not so much as the very smell of it; and God is our Warrant for what we say.

* * *

Soon after I had found my master . . . he authorized me to initiate a certain man of letters who had been one of my teachers in Quranic reading. This man, following my example, wanted to become a disciple of my own master and kept

26. See p. 15, note 2.

on asking me to obtain permission for him to do so. When I spoke to my master about it, he answered: "Take him by the hand yourself, since it was through you that he came to know about me." So I transmitted the teaching I myself had received and it bore fruit thanks to the blessing (*barakah*) inherent in my noble master's authorization. However, since I had to leave Fez in order to go back to the Banī Zarwāl tribe where I had left my parents, I was separated from him.

As for the master, he was still living in Fez al-Bālī and when I was about to set out on my journey to the tribe in question I said to him: "Where I am going there is no one at all with whom I could have spiritual conversation and yet I am in need of such exchange." He answered: "Beget the man you need!" as though he thought that spiritual generation could take place through me, or as though he already saw it. I spoke to him again on the same theme and again he replied: "Beget them!" Now, thanks to the blessing emanating from his authorization and from his secret,[27] a man came to me (may God multiply his like in Islam!) who, at the instant I saw him and he me, was filled by God to overflowing, to such a degree that he attained in one leap the spiritual station (*maqām*) of extinction (*fanā'*) and subsistence (*baqā'*) in God; and God is our Warrant for what we say. In this very event, the virtue and secret power contained in authorization[28] were revealed to me and all doubts or suggestions left me, thanks and praise be to God!

27. *Sirr*, that is, the secret of his spiritual rank, known only to God.

28. Spiritual authorization (*idhn*) includes two inseperable aspects: it dispenses with individual initiative, causing the one authorized to become the instrument of supra-individual will and at the same time transmits a blessing or spiritual power which acts by virtue of this instrumentality.

Later, my soul desired to receive the authorization of God Himself and of His Messenger (God bless him and give him peace). I aspired to this most persistently. Now when one day I happened to be in a lonely spot in the midst of the forest and was immersed and overwhelmed in extreme spiritual intoxication and at the same time in extreme sobriety—both aspects exceedingly powerful—all of a sudden I heard these words sounding forth from the depths of my essence: *Urge them to remember, for remembrance profits the believers* (LI, 54).[29] Then my heart became calm and rested, because I knew for certain that these words were addressed to me by God and His Prophet (God bless him and give him peace), immersed as I was in the two generous Presences, the one Dominical, the other Prophetic.[30] What came about (but God knows best) was that the ordinary laws were broken, by a rupture proceeding from the very depths of my essence. Of course there can be no "how" and it can be known only by him to whom God makes it known . . .

No sooner had this authorization been given to me than the believers came toward me and no sooner did I see them and they me than they remembered (God) and we also remembered,[31] and we profited by them as they profited by us and there occurred what occurred in the way of divine favors, secrets, powers, blessings and help. All this

29. The word *dhikrā,* translated here as "remembrence" includes, like *dhikr,* the meanings "mention," "reminder," "invocation," but also "admonition."

30. Allusion to the Sufic doctrine of the various Divine Presences (*ḥaḍarāt*), which are so many universal revelations of God. The "Dominical (*rabbānī*) Presence" refers to God as revealed in His perfect and transcendent Qualities, whereas the "Prophetic Presence" refers to God as revealed in the universe.

31. In Arabic there is a play upon the double meaning of the word *dhikr.* See note 29, above.

came to pass amongst the Banī Zarwāl tribe (God safeguard it from all trials), praise and thanks be to God!

*
* *

For men whose spiritual station (*maqām*) is extinction (*fanā'*), the Divine Qualities are nothing but the Essence (*dhāt*) of God, for when these men are extinguished in God, they contemplate His Essence only; they no sooner contemplate It, than they see nothing outside of It; and this is why they are called *dhātiyyun* ("essential"). Now the Divine Essence possesses such Infinitude, such Beauty and Goodness that even the most perfect intelligences among the elect are bewildered, to say nothing of the majority; for It becomes so subtle and so fine that It vanishes because of excess of subtlety and fineness; and in that state, It says to Itself: My Infinitude, My Beauty, My Goodness, My Splendor, My Penetration, My Elevation, My Exaltation know no bounds. Thus It is unmanifested. But the Infinite is not infinite unless it is at the same time unmanifested and manifested, subtle and solid, near and distant, having simultaneously the qualities of beauty and severity, and so forth; now, when Essence wished to manifest all this, It wondered (while knowing quite well): How shall I manifest it? And It answered Itself: I shall reveal and veil Myself at the same time; and this is what It did. Hence the essences of things, or more exactly, the forms which, as such, are present or absent, subtle or solid, higher or lower, near or distant, spiritual or sensory, merciful or terrible. These are all Essence, or, if you prefer, forms in which the Beauty of the Essence is manifested, although they are unable to manifest the Essence as such, since in Itself there is nothing but Itself alone and there is nothing outside of It. On this subject, the Masters of the Way among our brothers in the East have said:

> Without any doubt,
> In the absence of doubt, the All is Beauty, the Beauty of God.
> Doubt's target is but the trace of nothingness.
> O thou who drinkest at the source (*ʿayn*), when thou shalt realize, doubt will cease.
> The Essence is the very essence and source (*ʿayn*)[33] of the Qualities;
> In this truth there is no doubt.

And many other words have been uttered with the same meaning by the Masters of the Way in the East and in the West. If you understand our allusions, *faqīr,* then may God bless you, and if not, take note of your quality in order that our Lord may expand you by His Quality. And know that Majesty is Essence, whereas Beauty is Qualities; but the Qualities are none other than the Essence, as they recognize who have attained the state of extinction, though the others do not, that is to say, our masters in outer knowledge. Now there is no doubt that the outer is pure severity *(al-jalāl),* whereas the inner is pure clemency *(al-jamāl).*[34] Yet the outer lends something of

33. *Adh-dhāt* is the Essence in the absolute meaning of the word, the ultimate reality to which all qualities relate; as for *al-ʿayn,* which is used here as a synonym of *ad-dhāt,* it means more exactly essential determination, archetype; at the same time, the word *ʿayn* includes the meaning 'source' and 'eye', which makes it even more suggestive in this context.

34. The divine Qualities can he divided into two groups relating respectively to Majesty *(al-jalāl)* and Beauty *(al-jamāl).* Majesty, the revelation of which burns and consumes the worlds, is in one aspect rigorous, severe, whereas Beauty is the synthesis of mercy, generosity, compassion and all analogous qualities. In Hinduism, Shiva and Vishnu have respectively the same functions. Earlier in this text, we translated *jalāl* and *jamāl* by "majesty" and "beauty"; in the present context, applied cosmically and psychologically, it is more suitable to speak of "severity," "clemency," and so on.

its severity to the inner, just as the inner lends some of its clemency to the outer, so that the outer becomes clement severity and the inner severe clemency. However, the outer severity is real and its clemency only borrowed; just as the inner clemency is real, its severity only borrowed. Only he knows this who, as we have done, has studied esoteric knowledge deeply, has submerged himself and been extinguished, as we have been submerged to the point of extinction. (May God be well pleased with us).

Hear, *faqīr,* what the venerable Master and Saint Abū ᶜAbd-Allāh Muhammad ibn Aḥmad al-Anṣārī as-Sāḥili says in his book entitled *The Supreme Aim of the Spiritual Traveller in the Noblest of Ways.*[35] "Know (and may God illumine our hearts with the light of gnosis and lead us on the path of all holy gnostics) that gnosis is the degree of *iḥsān*[36] and the last step of the gnostic. God (be He exalted) said: *They have not valued God according to his right measure* (XXII, 73), that is to say, they have not truly known Him. He also says: *Thou wilt see how their eyes overflow with tears because of what they perceive of the Truth.* (V, 86). And the Prophet says: 'The pillar is the support of the house and the pillar of the just is the knowledge of God.' Now we understand by gnosis (*maᶜrifah*) the fixing of contemplation in a state of sobriety, accompanied by the exercise of justice and wisdom; and this is something quite different from the definition of knowledge

35. *Bughyat as-sālik fi ashraf al-masālik.*

36. *al-iḥsān*: contemplative virtue, defined by this saying of the Prophet: "Worship God as if you saw Him; if you do not see Him, nevertheless He sees you."

(*maʿrifah*) given by doctors of the Law, who see nothing beyond the knowledge of dogma. Although in principle gnosis includes all knowledge, including therefore theological knowledge insofar as it is knowledge, nevertheless the knowledge of God is distinct from all other knowledge because it concerns the significance of the Divine Names and Qualities, not in an analytical way, but without any separation between the Qualities and the Essence. This is the knowledge which gushes from the spring of union, which is derived from perfect purity and which comes to light by dwelling unceasingly in intimate consciousness with God (may He be exalted) . . ." Finally he says: "If this is acquired, then gnosis is none other than the highest degree of initiates and the goal of those who travel toward God, and this is the quality in which they give their selves in exchange for God. And even if nothing is left of them but their name alone, still we will speak of their states and their condition so that you may know, thanks to that, the whole extent of what we have failed to obtain from God (may He be exalted) and so that you may follow that way on which the solitary ones have gone before you, in which the gnostics have been victorious, while the limited ones, the men of outer knowledge, reject it. *Truly we belong to God and to Him we return* (II, 155)."

* * *

Intention is surely the true elixir, for this is what gave me strength when I was searching for him who would lead me toward God and I found him right there in front of me, quite near; it was almost as though he were living in the same house.[37]

My Master (God be satisfied with him) was outwardly all rigor, inwardly all beauty; I mean to say that outwardly he practiced abasement and servitude, while inwardly being glory and freedom. And what could be worse than the other way round, that is, a state of outward glory and freedom which inwardly is abasement and slavery; or outwardly traditional, inwardly innovation; outwardly in accorddance with law, inwardly lawless; lordly in appearance,

37. Al-ʿArabi ad-Darqāwī gave an account of his first meeting with his master, which is related by his disciple Ibn al-Khayyaṭ in the printed edition of the collected letters:

"That night I asked God to confirm my intention (of becoming a disciple of the Master ʿAlī al-Jamal), and I spent the whole night picturing him to myself, wondering what he was like and how my meeting with him would be, unable to sleep. When morning came, I went to find him at his Zāwiyah in the Rumaylah quarter, located between the two cities (of Fez), on the river bank, in the direction of the Qiblah, on the very spot where his tomb lies today. I knocked on the gate and there he was before me, sweeping out the Zāwiyah—as was his custom, for he never gave up sweeping it every day with his own blessed hand, in spite of his great age and high spiritual function. "What do you want?" he said. "O my Lord," I replied, "I want you to take me by the hand for God." Then he began to reprove me furiously, hiding his true state from my eyes, with words such as these: "And who told you that I take anyone at all by the hand and why ever should I do so for you?" And he drove me away—all to test my sincerity. So I went away. But when night came I questioned God once more (by means of the Holy Book). Then after performing the morning prayer, I went back again to the Zāwiyah. I found the master again sweeping as before and knocked at the gate. He opened it and let me in and I said: "Take me by the hand, for God's sake !" Then he took me by the hand and said: "Welcome!" He led me into his dwelling place in the inner part of the Zāwiyah and manifested great joy. "O my Lord," I said to him, "I have been looking for a master for so long !" "And I," he replied, "was looking for a sincere disciple."

satanic underneath? "Nothing so impedes progress to the end (of the Way) as the fact of having neglected the foundations."[38] There is no doubt: when men of the elect, such as my master and his like, humble themselves outwardly and of their own accord, God raises them up both inwardly and outwardly, so that they live in perpetual joy, whereas ordinary men, when they do the opposite, that is to say when they glorify themselves outwardly, are brought low by God, both outwardly and inwardly, so that they live in constant unhappiness.

Our master was content with his knowledge of God and turned neither toward what is manifested nor toward what is hidden; he had regard only for his relationship with God and had no care for the praise or blame of others. Thus he often recited these verses:

> Mayest Thou deign to be sweetness and let life be bitter!
> If Thou art content, what matter that men be angry.
> Let everything between me and Thee be cultivated,
> Between me and the worlds may all be desert!
> If Thy love be assured, all is then easy,
> For everything on earth is but earth."

His very way of being expressed: O God, may my shame be visible to the eyes of created beings, my wholeness visible to Thee, and not the reverse! God, be He exalted, has said: *They (men) in no way make thee independent of God.* (XLV, 19).

Hear, *faqīr,* some of my Master's sayings (may God be well pleased with him): "While other people are busy with worship, do you pay heed to Him who is worshipped; when they are busy with love, do you be busy with the

38. Sufi proverb.

Beloved; while they are seeking to perform miracles, do you look for the delights of prayer; while they multiply their devotions, attend to your most generous Lord," and so forth. He also used to say in the course of spiritual conversation: "If you contemplated Him in everything, contemplation of Him would veil all things from your sight. For He is the only thing outside of which there is no thing.— If you bring together the ephemeral and the eternal, the ephemeral is extinguished and the eternal alone subsists.— If the qualities of the Well-Beloved were to be manifested, both the veil and he whose sight is veiled would be as naught.—When the lights of pure contemplation are revealed, both the abstainer and that from which he abstains disappear.—To abstain from things is to overestimate their power and this is due to the veil that hides God from you; for if you contemplated Him in things (as they arise), or before or after (things), they would not hide Him from you. It is because you are preoccupied with things that God is hidden from you by them; if you saw their existence as flowing from Him, their existence would not hide Him from you.—The only thing that comes between you and Him whom you worship is joy in what you have and regret for what you do not have; the only thing that separates you from bliss is this faulty quality.—Were it not for the plotter and the spy[39] your joy in the Beloved could not become perfect. Were it not for the fire and the bee sting, one would not be able to taste the comb and the honey."[40] And so forth.

39. This is an allusion to the hostility of the human world, and also to psychic interference.

40. In Arabic, all these aphorisms are in the form of rhymed couplets.

He also said: "He lies who claims to have drunk the wine of the initiates and to have understood their spiritual truths, yet does not detach himself from the world. Just as Paradise is not accessible to him who has not died and been reborn, so is the Paradise of Gnosis closed to him whose soul is not dead to the world, to the desire to act in it, to choose, to possess and enjoy it—who is not dead to everything except God."

He also said (may God be well pleased with him): "Do not say 'I' before having been extinguished (in God). You will have no life before having undergone death.—The suns will not rise in you until after the death of the souls.[41]—You will not reach the goal you desire so long as people still have praises for you.—You will not taste the food of faith until you come out from the created worlds.[42]—You will reach extinction (*fanā'*) only after having died to the evanescent world.—If the veils were to be torn asunder for you, you would contemplate the Beloved in yourself.—If the suggestions of imagination were to cease, you would contemplate the eternal without ceasing.—If your soul did not take you away from Him, you would see no reality except your Lord.—If your soul were freed of filth, the Truth would come and vanity would disappear."[43]

*
*   *

41. In this aphorism, "suns" and "souls" in the plural is an allusion to the many degrees to be gone through on the spiritual path, each new "illumination" being preceded by the death of a "soul."

42. According to the Qur'ān, faith *(al-īmān)* can increase to an unlimited extent; therefore, in its higher degrees, it is identical with gnosis.

43. This is an allusion to the verse in the Qur'ān: *Truth has come and vanity has disappeared, for vanity is by nature bound to disappear.* (XVII, 81).

. . . If you wish to free yourself from your passionate soul, reject what it tries to suggest to you and pay no attention to it, for it will most certainly continue to molest you and will not leave you in peace; it will say to you, for example: you are lost! Let its insinuations neither disturb nor dismay you, whatever it may say, but remain seated, if you were seated, or standing, if you were standing; continue to sleep if you were sleeping, to eat if you were eating, to drink if you were drinking, to laugh if you were laughing, to pray if you were praying or to recite if you were reciting, and so on. Do not listen to it, unless it says to you: you belong to the believers, to those who know God, or: you are in the hand of God and His grace and His generosity are without measure. For it will not cease to harass you with its whisperings until you become fixed in impassivity toward it, as we have recommended, while continuing to conform to the wont (*sunnah*) of the Prophet; but if you do listen to it, it will begin by saying: you are going to lose, then you are an evildoer! and, if unbelief were not the very limit of the trial,[44] it would say to you: you are an unbeliever! and go on accusing you more and more.

*
* *

There is nothing more conducive to concentration of the heart on God than silence and fasting, just as there is nothing more conducive to dispersion than too much food and too many words, even about what concerns us.

*
* *

44. He who does not believe in transcendent reality cannot be tried; he feels comfortable in his earthly dream.

Know (may God be merciful to you) that the Masters of the way whose state combines rapture (*jadhb*) and method (*sulūk*)—and one can equally well say: intoxication and sobriety—are the true intermediaries between us and our Lord, and not those who have method without being enraptured or who are enraptured without method, or rather, in other terms: who are intoxicated without sobriety or sober without intoxication. He who adheres to the true intermediaries is saved and he who is against them drowns, for the Sufis have said that he who has no Master has Satan for master.

* * *

The sickness that is afflicting your heart is one of those things which strike men whom God loves, for "of all men the most sorely tried are the Prophets, after them the saints, then those who resemble them, closely or remotely."[45] So do not be downcast, since this happens most often to men full of sincerity and love, to cause them to go forward toward their Lord. By this suffering their hearts are purified and transformed into pure substance. Lacking such encounters with reality, nobody would reach the knowledge of God, far from it, for "if there were no arenas for souls, the runners would not be able to run their course" as it is said in Ibn ᶜAṭā-Illāh's *Ḥikam,* in which he also says: "In the variety of signs and changing states I came to recognize Thine intention in regard to me, that of showing me all things, so that there might be nothing in which I would not know Thee." In the same sense, the initiates have said:

45. Saying of the Prophet.

"It is in times of upheaval that men stand out from amongst men." In the Qur'ān it is said: *Do the people then reckon that they will be left in peace because they say 'we believe,' and that they will not be tried?* (XXIX, 1).

Hear also what has been related about the attitude of those who know God: when our Lord ᶜUmar ibn ᶜAbd al-Azīz[46] (may God be well pleased with him) was asked: "What do you wish?" he answered: "Whatever God decides." The illustrious Master, our Lord ᶜAbd al-Qādir al-Jīlānī, said on this subject:

> It is not my part, if trials come my way, to turn away from them,
> Nor, if I am flooded with joy, to abandon myself to it;
> For I am not of those who, for the loss of one thing, are consoled
> By another; I wish nothing less than the All.

And the renowned Master Ibn ᶜAtā-Illāh says in his *Ḥikam*: "May the pain of trial be lightened for you by your knowledge that it is He, be He exalted, who is trying you." There is no doubt that, for men of God, their best moment is the moment of distress, for this is what fosters their growth. He also says in his *Ḥikam:* "The best of your moments is that in which you are aware of your distress and thrown back upon your own helplessness . . . it may be that in distress you will find benefits that you have been unable to find either in prayer or in fasting." Distress (*fāqah*) is nothing but intensity of need. Now our Master's Master, al-ᶜArabī Ibn ᶜAbd-Allāh, called distress "incitement," because

46. The Caliph ᶜUmar II (d. 720 A.D.), whose brief but godly reign is always looked on as a throw-back to the golden age of the first four caliphs.

it incites him who is afflicted to go forward on the way toward his Lord. And our own Master (may God be well pleased with him) said: "If people knew how many secrets and benefits are to be found in need, they would have no other need than to be in need." And he said likewise that distress takes the place of the Supreme Name (of God). On the other hand, he considered power to be a limitation.

From another point of view, we observe that the knowledge of God turns trials aside from us, as it did for the Prophets (on them be prayer and peace) and the Saints. God, be He exalted, says in the Qur'ān: *We said to the fire: O fire, be coolness and protection for Abraham. They set a trap for him, but we made them the losers and saved him* (XXI, 69–71). God also said: *And it is said to those who fear (God): what did God bring down? They answer: that, which is good* (XVI, 30); and this in spite of the fact that God "brings down" the great trials on them alone, out of love for them and attention to them, as it is said in the glorious Qur'ān: *How many Prophets had fighting beside them numbers of men of the Lord, men who did not falter for the hardships they suffered in the way of God* (III, 145), and again: *If ye have received a wound, be sure that the people received just such a wound* (before you)" (III, 140). And so forth. However, their knowledge of God and their absorption in contemplating the infinity of His essence makes them indifferent to good and to evil; their look is turned only upon their Lord; just as they see Him in rejoicing, so do they see Him in grief, since He is at the same time the cause of rejoicing (*al-munʿim*) and of punishment (*al-muntaqim*); or it might be said: just as they contemplate Him in the gift, so do they contemplate him in privation.

As the illustrious Master Ibn ʿAṭā-Illāh says in his *Ḥikam:* "When He gives, He causes you to contemplate His kindness and when He withholds He shows you His victorious power *(qahr); He* it is throughout who makes Himself known to you and who, in His mercy (*luṭf*), comes closer to you." In a word, for such men God is qualified at once by terrible majesty (*jalāl*) and by kindness (*jamāl*); as for trials they know nothing of them, nor do trials know them, since they strike only those who are under the veil and not those for whom the veil has been drawn back; for the cause of trial is the existence of the veil and the perfection of enjoyment is nothing but the sight of the Face of God, the All-Generous. All grief and sorrow that hearts experience comes only from being cut off from the essential vision, as Ibn ʿAṭā-Illāh says in his *Ḥikam*.

*
* *

Imagination (*wahm*) is a vain thing, but God ordained it with great wisdom in view. Indeed, each thing bears at the same time a great secret and an aspect which is evident, for it is said (in the Qur'ān): *Our Lord, Thou didst not create that in vain, be Thou exalted* (III, 191). And: *Do ye then think We created you in sport?* (XXIII, 117). Far be such a thing from our Lord. God is above that. It is in the nature of imagination that if you do not bring it under your yoke, that is, impose your way of thinking upon it, it will inevitably dominate you and impose its own way on you; if you do not deny its opinion, it will deny yours. Now, it is nothing; yet, if you listen to its talk, it will weaken your (spiritual) certainty and will turn you away from that into other paths. But if you do not listen to what it says, your inner light will increase; by its increase your certainty will be strengthened; as this becomes stronger, your spiritual will arises and by its arising you will reach your Lord, and to reach Him is to know Him.

For travellers toward God who neither listen to imagination's talk nor go by its opinions, it is like a powerful wind that comes to the aid of sailors and causes them to arrive in an hour where others arrive only after a month's or a year's voyage. On the other hand, a man who stops to listen to the talk and opinions (of imagination) remains held up on the way, just as it happens to sailors. This is the effect it has.[47]

We see that he who gives up what does not concern him is able to subsist with next to nothing, whereas he who does not will never have all he requires, do what he may.

* * *

All good lies in the remembrance (*dhikr*) of God, since He said (be He exalted): *For men and women who remember God often, God has prepared forgiveness and a great reward* (XXIII, 35). He also said: *Remember Me and I will remember you*[48] and, *Give thanks to Me and be not unbelievers* (II, 152). Likewise: *Woe unto them whose hearts are hardened against the*

47. As a creative faculty of the soul, imagination may be receptive either in regard to the "world" or in regard to spiritual truths. It is not that the worldly man's imagination is too powerful; quite the contrary, what characterizes him is the imagination which is carried away and fettered by the objects of his desires.

48. Or: *Mention Me and I will mention you (idhkurūnī adhkurkum).* The verb *dhakara,* from which the noun *dhikr* is derived, has the inclusive meaning: to remember, to mention, to call upon.

mention (dhikr) of God; those are in manifest error (XXXIX, 22). The Prophet (on him be peace) made known to us these divine words[49]: "I am near to him who calls upon Me." Let that suffice to show the excellence of remembrance and the fault in forgetfulness.[50] And if the divine words we have quoted were not enough for us, then nothing would be enough and there would be no good in us. God promises an immense reward to those who remember and indeed we have no need of anything other than that. All we need is to go against our passionate desires,[51] for by that we acquire intuitive knowledge, which in turn gives us the great certainty, and the great certainty will deliver us from all doubts and cares and will lead us toward the presence of the infinitely knowing King. There is no divinity but He.

Greetings of Peace.

*
* *

I would like you not to be scattered in your love, for that will prevent you from reaching the secret, the object of your desire, virtue and grace. We see that some people become attached now to one thing, now to another. They are like a man who tries to find water by digging a little here and a little there and will die of thirst; whereas a man who digs deep in one spot, trusting in the Lord and relying on Him, will find water[52]; he will drink and give others

49. *Ḥadith qudsī:* see p. 17, note 6.

50. *Ghaflah*: "forgetfulness," "negligence," as against *dhikr*, "remembrance," "invocation."

51. Which is at the same time a condition and an effect of the *dhikr*.

52. The same parable is to be found in the sayings of Sri Ramakrishna.

to drink (but God knows best). The Sufis used to say: knock persistently at one door and many doors will be opened to you; submit to one Master and the multitude will submit to you.

In the same way, a man who longs now for the East, now for the West,[53] travelling sometimes in one direction, sometimes in the other, who is sometimes moderate, sometimes greedy, is far from the goal; if he attained to nearness, he would stop his agitation and be at peace.

He who stops at opinion never arrives at realization. So cease to be busy with conjecture and never judge anything[54] on the basis of your individual opinion, but only after having realized it. For sincerity in deed and word destroys doubts and cares and strengthens consciousness of divine Unity (*tawḥīd*) in the heart of him who practices it constantly. It even causes the interference of the passionate soul (*nafs*) to disappear; and when the soul ceases to be hostile in a man, the hostility of the human collectivity toward him ceases also.[55] From that moment, it is his turn to act and God (be He exalted) will help him. But if he abstains from offending the servants of his Lord, while himself accepting their offences, he will be even greater in virtue and in spirituality, for this is the state of those of the saints who attain perfection.

Greetings of Peace.

53. The directions respectively of light and of darkness.

54. That is to say, judgment concerning something of a spiritual nature.

55. That is, when there ceases to be any egoism in a man, conscious or unconscious, then there is no target for hostility from his surroundings.

*
* *

An-nafs (the soul) and *ar-rūḥ* (the Spirit) are two names for one and the same thing, which is made of the very essence of light (But God is wiser). It divides into two by virtue of two opposite qualities, namely, purity and confusion. For, so long as it exists, the *nafs* is confused, and this is why it bears its name. But if its confusion disappears and it becomes pure substance, it is truly called *rūḥ*. We see besides that they mutually attract one another, because they are close to one another, and in principle both are endowed with beauty, virtue and balance. Now if God wishes to sanctify one of His servants, he marries Spirit and soul within him; that is, he causes one to take possession of the other; this comes about when the soul returns from the passions which had taken it far from its true kindred and from its country and torn it away from its virtue, its goodness, its beauty, its nobility, its higher nature, its exaltation and from everything with which its Lord had filled it, to the point of denying its own source and no longer being able to search for it. Now if the soul does not remain in this state, but leaves it and returns from it entirely, the Spirit transports it and transmits to it its truths and secrets, which God inspires and which are endless. The emanation of the Spirit from its Lord becomes stronger to the exact degree that the passions are forsaken, so that the marriages of Spirit and soul multiply, as do their fruits—intuitive knowledge and the actions springing from that knowledge. Rejoicing in this state is such that man can bear it only in going against the (passionate) soul and mastering it by means of what it hates and finds a burden; for he despises all that (part of the soul) and masters it easily, thanks to the light, the secrets and excellencies he sees in it.

* * *

Contemplation is intuition and intuition can only be made stable by means of the sensory; it endures only through spiritual conversation, visits to saints and the breaking of habits.[56] As soon as there is stagnation, contemplation inevitably ceases. Therefore do not stop your movements—I mean the actions by which contemplation is intensified. Our Master (may God be well pleased with him) used often to say to me: "Intuition is very subtle and volatile; if a man is not on guard, he does not notice when it escapes from his hands."

* * *

There is no reality (*mawjūd*) but God, be He exalted: *All things perish save His face* (XXVIII, 88); *Everything on the earth is passing away; your Lord's face alone abideth, essence of majesty and of generosity* (LV, 26–27); *Such is God your Lord, and what is there after Truth but error?* (X, 32); *It is thus because God is the Truth and what they invoke apart from Him is vanity* (XXII, 62); *Say: Truth has come and vanity has disappeared; most surely, vanity is bound to disappear* (XVII, 81); *Say Allāh,*

56. In other words, intuition can only be "fixed" in a symbol and can only be maintained by frequenting spiritual men (Sanskrit *satsanga*), by the influence emanating from living Saints or from the tombs of Saints, and by struggling against the passive habits of the soul.

then let them amuse themselves with idle chatter (VI, 91); *He is the First and the Last, the Outer and the Inner* (LVII, 3).

The Prophet (may God bless him and give him peace) has said: "I have seen nothing without seeing God in it"; and we say: it is impossible to see our Lord while seeing anything other than Him; and all who have reached this degree of knowledge affirm the same.

> I have known God and I see none other than Him,
> So that the "other" in us is shut out.
> Since I realized unity, I no longer fear separation;
> This day I have arrived, am united.

This means (but God knows more): I have known my Lord through contemplative and essential knowledge, not only through induction and rational proof, and since then I see Him alone in everything, as did the Prophet. As for the phrase: "since I realized unity I no longer fear separation," it means: I have seen unity in multiplicity, so that I am no longer afraid to see multiplicity in unity, as I was before coming to see my Lord in everything. Without any doubt, there is no reality apart from God; imagination (*wahm*) alone veils Him from our eyes and imagination is illusory. In this sense, the venerable Master and Saint Ibn ʿAṭā-Illāh says in his *Ḥikam:* "If the veil of imagination were torn away, essential vision would take place, annihilating all individual vision, and the rising light of certainty would veil all relative existence." Our Master al-Majdhūb says likewise:

> My sight was extinguished in a vision;
> I fainted away from every vanishing thing.
> I realized Truth and found nothing other than Him,
> And I am at peace in a state of bliss.

So do not imagine that there is something "with" God, for God alone is with God, as all those who have arrived at realization bear witness; only he who has not travelled this path does not know it.

*
* *

Have no fear of psychic suggestions when they assail you and flood your heart in waves ceaselessly renewed, but inwardly abandon all will to God and remain calm; do not be agitated, relax and do not be tense; and sleep, if you can, until you have your fill of it, for sleep is beneficial in times of distress; it brings marvelous benefits, for it is in itself abandonment to the divine will. Now, whoever abandons his will to his Lord, God takes him by the hand. Therefore do not be afraid of psychic suggestions when they increase, but be as we have said and you will profit by it—God's curse be on him who lies to you! As a result of such tribulations, consciousness of unity will be established in your hearts and doubts and imaginations will leave you alone; and thus you will progress in the way and will reach that good state which is the cessation of all error and liberation from it. And see that you do not become troubled by the many obstacles and impediments, for the good (may God strengthen it) will bend them in your favor if you persevere in what we have been telling you. A certain scholar said to me one day: "It is carnal desire that does me harm." To which I answered: "This is precisely what does me good. I am filled with the benefits of God and with the benefits of desire and, by God, I shall always be grateful to Him for it!" Men with knowledge of God do not run away from things as others do, for they contemplate their Lord in everything. The others run away because the sight of existing things prevents them from seeing Him from whom existence flows. About this, the illustrious Master Ibn ʿAṭā-Illāh says in his *Ḥikam:* "Devout men and ascetics cut themselves off from all things only because they find that things cut them off from God; if they contemplated Him in all things, they would not cut themselves off" . . .

And know (God be merciful to you) that nothing prevents us from contemplating our Lord but the fact of being preoccupied with the desires of our souls. Do not say that it is existence which veils the maker of existence, for, by God, it is imagination (*wahm*) alone that hides Him from us, the imagination which gives rise to ignorance.[59] If we only knew, it would lead us to the knowledge of certainty[60] and certainty would distract our heart and inmost consciousness from the sight of ephemeral things.

* * *

Hear what I said to one of our brothers to give him courage. He was afraid to marry because of the temptations that marriage would entail, as many of our people have been afraid. So I said to him: "We see that there are some men who, though not of the elect, yet manage to live in

59. This refers, not to imagination as a mere plastic mental faculty, but as that which attributes to things a reality they do not possess—"seeing the snake in the rope" as the Hindus say.

60. *ʿIlm al-yaqīn,* an allusion to the three degrees of intuitive knowledge designated by the Quranic terms: *ʿilm al-yaqīn* (knowledge of certainty); *ʿayn al-yaqīn* (eye of certainty), *ḥaqq al-yaqīn* (truth of certainty). See Abu Bakr Sirāj ad-Dīn: *The Book of Certainty.*

the midst of manifold occupations as though they had none, whereas others, responsible for nothing but their own head, befuddle it to the point of being always in great trouble. This comes from the fact that they are forever making plans and burdening themselves with a thousand worries. And so it appears to me (but God knows best) that grown men[61] do not allow themselves to be distracted from their Lord by anything at all and that concern for a family is the least of things. On what then does he rely, he amongst you who aspires to union and to that end gives up all activity for profit in this world or in the other? Is there anything more astonishing than that a man should put all the blame on his professional activity for not being able to perfect himself? He says: "If only I had abandoned my business and given all my attention to my Lord, I should be better off"; and yet there are many lost moments in his life; he does not see them and finds nothing wrong in the fact that he wastes these moments without a thought for his Master. This is where he goes astray and is lost, because it is not fitting that he should blame his business for having caused him to neglect the salvation of his soul and that of his family so long as, in his free moments, he is not paying the Lord his due."

Peace be on you.

* * *

I was teaching children in the *ᶜUyūn* quarter (the quarter of the springs) in Fez, reciting the glorious Qur'ān while

61. *rijāl, pl.* of *rajul,* literally "man" (as opposed to an adolescent or a woman) and used by the Sufis to denote spiritual Virility.

the children in front of me were reading from their tablets, when all of a sudden I saw myself in a boat on the sea near the city of Tunis (God protect it), reciting the Qur'ān just as I had been reciting it in school before the children. All the people on the boat were happy listening to my recitation. And just then many Christian boats appeared and came at us to take us captive. Seeing this, all those who were with me in the boat clung to me, for in their eyes I was truly a saint. Then God covered over my quality with His, so that I urged the boat toward the boats of the enemy, enveloping them in my violent power and my concentration. Some of them sank, others were shattered, others were captured; God is victorious over His creation.[62] After that I saw myself back in my school and I was like one sick or under a spell and as though someone had beaten my bones with iron bars. When I told my master what had happened, he put his hand over his mouth, then smiled and said: "Well, well, nobody knows where the rank of *quṭb* (spiritual pole, axis) is to be found—in the mountains herding goats or in school teaching children." Soon after, the news of what had happened came to Fez. God's curse be on those who lie!

*
* *

When my master saw that I was sincerely following the Way, he ordered me to break my soul's habits; he said to

62. It may be wondered why, toward the end of his collection of letters, Shaykh ad-Darqāwī relates a series of miraculous happenings concerning himself. In general, the Sufis are not in the habit of referring to their own charisma. No doubt his intention was to show in this way that the manifestations of grace inherent in the Way were no less effective than at the time of the great Sufis of the Middle Ages.

me: "Just as we have to acquire knowledge of spiritual reality (*al-ḥaqīqah*), so do we have to acquire the practice of it."

I did not understand. Then he took hold of my *ḥā'ik*[63] with his noble hand, plucked it off my head, twisted it several times and wound it round my neck.[64] And he said: "This is the test of what is good!" At that, my soul was so troubled that it would rather have died than be seen in such a ridiculous get-up. The master looked at me without saying a word and I felt oppressed to the point of death. I stood up before my master had risen to his feet—which was not my custom—walked away until the wall of the Zāwiyah hid me from his sight. Then my soul said to me: "Whatever does this mean?" I did not know how to answer unless by putting my *ḥā'ik* back over my head like other people—but no, I did not do it. Instead, I said to it: "The master knows very well what this means. But, soul of mine, why were you so shocked and disgusted? Why so afraid of being humiliated? Whatever are you and what is your station that you cannot bear to be in this condition? Do you then care for nothing except to remain with your lusts and comforts and to play around without restraint? No, by God, you are not going to enjoy yourself like that so long as I am there to watch over you and your hostile ways!" Then, seeing my eyes hot with anger, it gave up hope of getting what it lusted for and knew it would have none of it. At long last, it accepted the law I imposed upon it.

63. The *ḥā'ik* is a piece of cloth without a seam, used to cover the head and shoulders.

64. For a Muslim who has not come under modern Western influence, to allow himself to be seen in public bare-headed is a sign of vulgarity, lack of discipline or madness.

Woe to the *faqīr,* woe to him, if he sees the form of his own soul (or of his ego—*nafs*) just as it is, and does not strangle it until it dies!

*
* *

One morning I was performing the dawn prayer near the tomb of Aḥmad bin Yūsuf (may God allow us to profit through him), fearing the while lest the local people might do some harm to the *fuqarā'* in whom then prevailed a state of spiritual expansion (*basṭ*), whereas the world at that time was sunk in indifference toward God, and in injustice; few were they who defended God's cause.

Just then one of the *fuqarā'* came running up in terror, no doubt to tell me that what I feared had come to pass. He reached me just as I was reciting the words: *Perform the prayer, give alms and hold fast to God, who is your Protector. He is the best Protector and Helper* (XXII, 78). At that moment all the fear with which I had been filled left me and made room for hope and a great certainty; so I said to this *faqīr*—before he spoke to me: "The blow missed its mark; no harm will come to us. All the same, tell me what happened." Whereupon he told me how the villagers had connived together to write a letter accusing our brothers, the *fuqarā'* (God have mercy on them and on ourselves) of having done abominable things; the letter was to be sent to the regional governor and forwarded by him to the Sultan himself, who at that time was Muhammad bin ʿAbd Allah bin Ismāʿīl al-Ḥasanī al-ʿAlāwī (God have mercy on him). This news did not disturb me; I remained at ease, quietening myself while waiting for the day to dawn, when another *faqīr* arrived, even more frightened than the first, for, when he left, the people had fully decided to carry out their plan. He complained about it to me, saying "Here are these people intent on committing a great injustice toward their neighbors and you are doing nothing for us!" To this I replied: "What would you wish me to do? Would you like me to turn your village upside down?" As I said this, I made a movement with my hand as though to overturn something. And just as I did this, a man ran up from the village, sent by those villagers who so lately had been wishing to do us harm, He told me that a messenger had been on the way from Tangier, sent by the Pasha ᶜAbd aṣ-Ṣādiq ar-Rīfī to the governor Aḥmad bin Nāṣir al-ᶜAyyāshī in Taza, with a load of ten quintals of goods belonging to the Sultan himself, and having on him the sum of seventy *mithqāl* of his own; the messenger, it appeared, had been attacked and wounded near the village and left with blood all over his clothes, while the load of goods belonging to the Sultan had disappeared and the messenger's own property also. It seemed that the messenger had said to the villagers: "It was you who did this to me, for if you had not been a party to it, they would never have been able to waylay me." Hearing this, the villagers had turned pale with fear. So I went to them and found them like that and worse. And we thanked God for having saved us from their wickedness and trickery.

Greetings of Peace.

*
* *

I was in Fez at the time of the dearth and was making my way from shop to shop for alms. It was the season of penury, rain, cold, mud, hunger and darkness, and my family was waiting for me like a nestful of little starving birds. And along came a nobleman (*sharīf*) from amongst those who had more than enough, who shouted insults at me because I was begging and followed me from shop to shop, wherever I went, until nightfall. At last, night came and separated us and each of us went to his home. The first light of dawn had not yet appeared, when a man came looking for me on behalf of the nobleman's father and said to me: "So-and-so asks you to excuse him for disturbing you and sends you this message: 'For the love of God, come with the *fuqarā'* and be present at my son's burial, may God have mercy on him'." So we went to his burial. God be merciful to him as to ourselves.

Greetings of Peace.

* * *

When I was under a vow of devoting myself to spiritual poverty and was stripping myself of various conventions that are pleasing to people but of no value in themselves, my family and other people detested me, since instead of conforming to their ways I was becoming detached from them. Now, while our relationship was still like this, there was a drought; we prayed to God to send us rain, but no rain came and the drought continued. One day, when I was present at a family gathering, my brother ʿAlī (God be merciful to him) said to me: "The friends of God are able to work miracles and here is the wheat dying, burnt up by the sun. If you are one of them, then ask God to make it rain or else give up this spiritual poverty and go back to your studies." I was silent and did not answer him. But he was not silent; he insulted me and bore down on me with all the weight of his resentment, and everyone present was delighted, for in their eyes I was on the wrong road and blind, for the simple reason that I was no credit to the family. This scene went on and I accepted it all patiently—and nobody can bear such a thing unless God is helping him or unless he cannot do otherwise—until my heart was broken; then I went out of the mosque where we had held our meeting. I looked up at the sky, which was clear except for a tiny little cloud just above us. Then I said, as some of the saints have said: "O my Lord, if You will not take pity on me, I shall end by being angry!" And then it happened that the little cloud above us spread out in the wind, to the south and to the north, before us and behind, and the rain began to fall with such violence that we were soaked by it, inside the mosque as well as outside; the water flooded the mosque in which we were gathered just as it flooded the fields and reached us from above and from below. This came about through the divine grace which covered over my powerlessness with Its power.

Greetings of Peace.

* * *

I was in a state which was a very intense combination of spiritual intoxication and sobriety as, one evening, I entered the mosque which contains the tomb of the *Ḥusaynī Sharīf*[65] Aḥmad aṣ-Siqallī[66] in Fez. It was just the hour of sunset and the muezzin was calling to prayer from the roof of the sanctuary. I was wearing an old *muraqqaᶜah* (a cloak made of pieces of cloth patched together) and on my head three caps, equally old, one on top of the other, for such was my inclination at the time.[67] Now into the depths of my consciousness there came the idea that I needed a fourth cap and at that very moment the muezzin came down with it from the roof, running and laughing. A stork, carrying this cap off to her nest, had let it fall on him. As he came toward me, laughing, with the cap in his hand, I said to him: "Give it to me, for God's sake, it is meant for me!" And seeing that I was already wearing three caps just like it, he gave it to me.

For men in a state of spiritual sincerity (*ṣidq*), it is always like that; everything which is manifested in their hearts immediately makes its appearance in the sensory world. God's curse be on those who lie!

* * *

65. That is, a descendant of the Prophet in the line of his grandson, al-Ḥusayn.

66. As-Siqallī means "the Sicilian," the family having emigrated from Sicily. Ahmad as-Siqallī, who lived in the 18th century, was the founder of a branch of the Shādhilī order, which assimilated some of the methods originating with the Naqshabandīs. The mosque where he is buried, which serves as a meeting place for members of the order, is still extant.

67. A state like that of the *Malāmatiyyah,* who follow the path of "blame" and intentionally incur the disapproval of the more exoteric members of their religion.

Lastly, my brother, I strongly advise you—"religion is sincere counsel"[68]—not to give up the remembrance (*dhikr*)[69] of your Lord, as He himself told you to do it, *standing, sitting and reclining* (Qur'ān IV, 104) and in all conditions, for we need nothing but that; we, you and every man, whoever he may be.

Listen to what I am about to say to you and do not forget it, do not take it lightly or let it go unheeded. In the course of the past fifty-five years or so, I have said to many a brother: every single man has any number of needs, but in reality all men need only one thing, which is truly to practice the remembrance of God; if they have acquired that, they will not want for anything, whether they possess it or do not possess it.

Long after having said that, I read, in the Imām Abu'l-Qāsim al-Qushayrī's commentary on the most beautiful names of God, that a disciple said to his master: "Master, what about food ?" The master answered: "God!" The disciple persisted: "We absolutely have to have food," to which the master rejoined: "We absolutely have to have God." Later on, I found these words in Ibn ᶜAṭā-Illāh's *Ḥikam:* "What can he find who has not found You? and what can he lack who has found You? Whoever is content with anything in exchange for You perishes, and whoever desires some other thing in place of You is lost."

Without fail, without fail, be constant in your remembrance of your Lord, as He ordained, and cling to your religion with all your strength; God will open the eyes of your

68. Saying of the Prophet.

69. It will be recalled that the word *dhikr,* translated in this case as "remembrance" includes the meanings of mention, invocation, *anamnesis* in the Platonic sense of the term.

intelligence and enlighten your inmost conscience. And beware lest you think that a man who truly remembers God could possibly not be content with that; do not believe it, for it is impossible.

Know (may God be merciful to you) that I was expecting one of my *faqīr* friends to ask me: "Where did you find this saying: 'Every single man has many needs but in reality all men need only one thing, which is truly to remember God; if they have acquired that, they will not want for anything, whether they possess it or do not possess it.'" Now, if I had been asked, I would have replied that in my youth, about ten months after I reached maturity,[70] all in one moment I pierced through to the presence of my Lord and lo and behold, I was no longer as I had been until then, for God put His power in the place of my powerlessness, His strength in the place of my weakness, His wealth in the place of my poverty, His knowledge in the place of my ignorance, His glory in the place of my lowliness. In other words, He covered over my quality with His, in such a way that I was He and no longer myself; in the words of God brought to us by the Prophet (may God bless him and give him peace): "My servant never ceases to come closer to me through voluntary devotions until I love him; and as soon as I love him, I am He."[71] Among

70. Maturity is reckoned to begin at puberty and to entail moral responsibility and the obligation to perform the rites prescribed for every Muslim.

71. The following version of this *ḥadith qudsi* (see p. 17, note 6) is more generally known: "My servant never ceases to come closer to Me through voluntary devotions until I love Him; and when I love him, I am the ear with which he hears, the eye with which he sees, the hand with which he grasps; and if he asks something of Me, I will certainly give it to him."

other things that were given to me, my knowledge deepened so greatly that if a thousand times a thousand questions[72] were put to me, I would know how to answer them rightly, for I have become like a candle giving out a light that would not diminish if all existing candles were to be lighted from it. And God is our Warrant for what we say; God is our Warrant for what we say; God is our Warrant for what we say.

* * *

72. This refers, of course, to questions concerning spiritual realities.